Linking cubes and the Learning of mathematics

Making algebraic structure and mathematical thinking accessible to learners of all ages

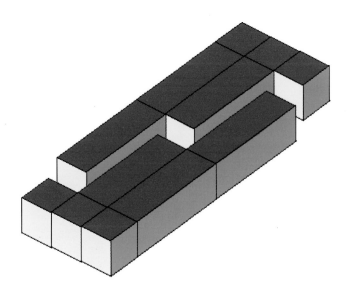

Paul Andrews

The Association of Teachers of Mathematics (ATM)

Published in April 2002 by ATM

Association of Teachers of Mathematics
7, Shaftesbury Street, Derby DE23 8YB
Telephone 01332 346599
Fax 01332 204357
e-mail admin@atm.org.uk

ISBN 1 898611 14 9

Copies may be purchased from the above address or www.atm.org.uk

About this book

What's in this book?

This book contains activities for the teaching of mathematics based on the use of linking cubes. The simplest and most cost-effective equipment a school can buy, linking cubes, as this book shows, can be used to offer learners concrete experiences of a wide range of mathematical ideas. These range from notions of pre-algebra through linear sequences and their general forms, non linear sequences, elementary number theory based on an analysis of triangular and square numbers, algebraic identities and techniques, to probability, sampling, permutations and combinations. In short, it is hoped that colleagues will find worthwhile uses for linking cubes irrespective of the age or alleged sophistication of their learners.

Why is it in this book?

It is my hope that this book will enable teachers at all levels to make productive and worthwhile use of linking cubes in their teaching. My experience is that most colleagues have a small repertoire of activities that they could use, but too often they don't, due to perceived threats to the smooth running of their classrooms. It is not without irony that one observes that where children use such materials regularly few such problems are likely to occur. Of course, the first time learners are given cubes to use, they make models of Tracey Island or My Little Pony. However, this reaction is not the preserve of the adolescent. Undergraduates, postgraduate teacher trainees, and teachers on in-service courses behave similarly; the only difference being that children's models are more sophisticated. Thus, this book aims to offer ideas that will allow linking cubes to be used regularly and meaningfully from upper primary through to undergraduate. In this way they become an everyday and accepted tool of the mathematics classroom which, therefore, helps prevent the claims made by many learners that they are the preserve of those younger or less talented than them.

What does this book contribute to mathematical understanding?

Much mathematics is about structure which is something that linking cubes can expose in ways that teaching based on, say, number patterns or algorithms is unlikely to achieve. Learners who understand, and have an aware of, structure will be more successful learners of, and see more purpose in, mathematics than those who do not. An understanding and awareness of structure will make transparent many mathematical results which otherwise, despite being visibly algebraically sound, remain opaque in terms of insight and understanding. Almost all of the activities encourage high level thinking and many have been included solely for the contribution they might make to children's understanding of, and ability to engage with, proof. A substantial number allude, although how transparently this is done will depend on the ways in which individual teachers chose to use them, to notions of mathematical induction and can be used as pre-inductive activities.

Many of the tasks could be viewed as simple investigations. However, the explicit focus on structure is intended to move learners' thinking beyond an inductive approach to mathematics - the systematic collection of numerical data from which generalities are inferred - to more deductive forms of argument. Additionally, many of the activities are clearly focused on learners' gaining access to conventional results of algebra and elementary number theory, although it is argued that the manner in which they are presented makes them accessible to younger learners than might ordinarily be the case.

What isn't in this book?

This isn't a book to be given to learners. The activities are not offered as worksheets to be copied but presented in ways that invite colleagues to work with them, explore them, gain ownership over them and then decide how they might use them and with whom. I know, for example, that an idea that works for me may need changing for someone else. I know, also, that the same activity, if altered slightly, will be appropriate for different ages and abilities. That is, my reasons for using any activity will vary according to particular circumstances - nothing is pre-determined and nor should it be. I don't know your classes and you don't know mine.

What is the teacher's role?

All the activities shown in this book expect colleagues to make some form of intervention. For many years the use of manipulatives (as things like linking cubes are more generically known) has received a poor press. This is almost entirely because teachers have assumed that just working with them will be sufficient for the learner to make sense of the task he or she has been given. Such assumptions are nonsensical. Teachers need to intervene, with individuals and with the class, in order to ensure that sense-making takes place. As indicated above, many of the activities have a simple script offered alongside them. This is intended as no more than a set of prompt questions to inform colleagues' sense-making of the task and preparation of their own scripts which will be focused on classes and individuals whom they know well.

Acknowledgements

This book has been simmering on the back burner for nearly fifteen years. During that time a number of trainee teachers and school-based colleagues with whom I've worked have asked why the ideas have never been brought together. The reason for not doing it has been, in essence, quite simple. I've always been reluctant to commit ideas to a book because my thinking changes frequently and there's something of permanence in the writing of a book which makes me feel uneasy. However, I hope that colleagues will find something of use in the following pages and that the activities will enhance their teaching and their students' learning.

The book would never have come to fruition without the support and encouragement of Heather Massey. It was her commissioning me to work with her department that finally led to the decision that colleagues might find a book helpful. She has worked with me for a number of years and her insightful comments and willingness to trial ideas with her pupil has helped immeasurably in bringing everything together in as coherent a way as possible.

I would also like to mention my appreciation of the support given me by Don Steward of Median publications - it was his suggesting, when we both worked for Shropshire LEA, that I work on these activities with school-based colleagues that convinced me that the ideas were worth developing further.

Lastly, I would like to thank colleagues on the General Council of the Association of Teachers of Mathematics, and in particular Mererid Stone, for their forbearance during the months these ideas were brought together on paper.

Cambridge University Faculty of Education

December 2001

Contents

Section 1

This first section presents a small number of activities focused on pre-algebra and simple notions of linear growth. They are intended to help learners see how, when linear growth occurs in a systemic way, some elements of a structure will remain constant (invariant) and others will change in a predictable and consistent manner. It is through such structural analyses that learners will learn to make statements about the general case.

1.1 Animals and the beginnings of algebra   1

1.2 Tee-shaped algebra   3

1.3 Caterpillar algebra   5

1.4 Ell-shaped algebra   7

Section 2

The second section takes a look at triangular numbers. It begins with a structural activity that leads to an awareness of the general form of the nth triangular number ($T_n = n(n+1)/2$) followed by a set of tasks that explore some of the fascinating, yet accessible, ideas that can be gleaned from them. It is in this section that we begin to see some of the delightful links between geometry and algebra and see how, for example, the sums of the cubes equates to the square of a triangular number.

2.1 The generalisation of triangular numbers   11

2.2 Some facts about triangular numbers   13

2.3 More facts about triangular numbers   15

2.4 Triangles from triangles   17

2.5 Some identities concerning triangular numbers   19

2.6 Cubes from triangles   25

2.7 More cubes from triangles   27

Section 3

The third section comprises a variety of tasks related to square numbers. It explores some of the algebraic identities concerning squares and their differences as well as some combinatorics tasks. It looks at squares as the sums of odd numbers and, significantly, offers a structural insight into the expression for the difference of two squares.

3.1 Squares and the sum of the odd numbers   29

3.2 Squares on squares   31

3.3 Squares from squares - difference of two squares   35

3.4 More squares from squares   37

3.5 Rectangles on rectangles   41

Section 4

The fourth section offers a range of activities focused, for the most part, on non-linear relationships. In particular it includes activities focused on the factorisation of quadratic expressions and a structural investigation of series derived from linear sequences. Included in this section is an explicit addressing of some of the issues concerning arithmetic progressions which makes accessible to younger pupils a mathematical topic normally taught only to older pupils.

4.1 Staircases and equivalent forms   43

4.2 Growing patterns   45

4.3 Spirals   47

4.4 The factorisation of quadratic expressions   49

4.5 Linear sequences and their series   53

Section 5

The fifth section comprises tasks covering a range of ideas from across the mathematics curriculum. Some explicitly scaffold children's work on surface area, others allow an early, and informal, engagement with mathematical induction. Some explicitly address some interesting, but accessible, number theoretic ideas that can be gleaned from summing consecutive integers.

5.1 A cubic problem	57
5.2 Frames from cubes	59
5.3 Closed-cornered circuits	61
5.4 The four cube and other problems	63
5.5 Surface area	65
5.6 Surface area and skeleton cubes	67
5.7 Trapezium numbers	69
5.8 Consecutive sums	73

Section 6

The sixth section focuses on a range of ideas concerning, for the most part, series and how their general forms might be accessed from an analysis of their structure. Most activities begin with some form of pyramid which is presented as a representation of the sum of particular shapes. Among these can be found the sums of the squares and the sums of the triangular numbers.

6.1 The skeleton tower	77
6.2 Square pyramids - sums of squares	79
6.3 Triangular pyramids - sums of triangular numbers	81
6.4 Generalising pyramids	83

Section 7

The last section differs from the others in its not focusing on structure, algebra or geometry but on the use of linking cubes as a context for work on probability and sampling. Amongst these is an activity that connects frequentist and classical conceptions of probability whilst another looks at sampling and how it might be undertaken in a purposeful manner. The final activity presents some tasks that facilitate children's ability to talk mathematically.

7.1 Talking mathematically   85

7.2 Probability   87

7.3 Sampling   89

7.4 Permutations and combinations   91

1.1 Animals and the beginnings of algebra

This well-known activity is presented here as one element of a set addressing notions of pre-algebra. Its intention is to alert learners, in an accessible and systematic way, to the idea that objects that grow in regular ways can be interpreted in terms of those components that change and those that remain constant. The manner in which the activity is described is intended to be indicative of the sorts of ways you might wish to use it and should not be seen definitive.

The pictures below show the first two of a set of animals.

 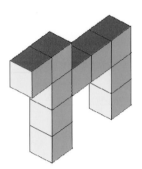

Imagine you were to ask your pupils to think about the third animal in the family. You could ask them to make it or you could ask them to consider the differences and similarities of the first two in order to make statements about its various properties. The latter could involve questions like:

- How many cubes will be needed for its head?

- How many cubes will be needed for its front leg?

- How many cubes will be needed for its hind leg?

- How many cubes will be needed for its body?

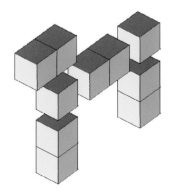

How does the picture on the left help in this process? Perhaps you could ask your pupils to find other ways of deconstructing the animal in order to show those parts of the body, which remain constant and those that vary.

It may make an interesting activity to ask all children to find at least two ways of doing it.

Of course, there are other families of animals you could build. We have no restrictions on what we do at times like this other than to make sure we offer pupils a sense that growth is systematic. For example, below are the first two of a second set of animals.

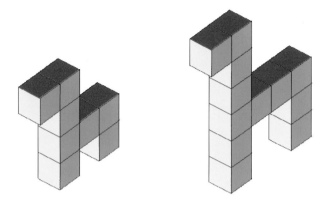

- Which of their components change, or are invariant?

- Which of their components change or are variable?

- How does such knowledge help in predicting the size of subsequent animals?

- How does it help in the process of generalisation?

Does the vocabulary one uses to describe the components of an animal help or hinder the processes of generalisation?

The success of activities like this depends on the ways that teachers, and their pupils, interact with the ideas and with themselves. Discussion and the sharing and resolving of different perspectives is an important aspect of work like this.

Having discussed the third animal, one might jump directly to the tenth and ask for details of its different body parts. This could take account of different deconstructions and show how they yield equivalent results and, ultimately, take the learner to a sense of the general with children describing, in oral terms, the properties of some unspecified, generalised, beast.

1.2 Tee-shaped algebra

The activity below is another in the set of pre-algebra tasks which offer learners opportunities to engage with invariance, variance and generality. Ideas for its development, which colleagues will need to explore in order to make it their own, are presented along with, it is hoped, helpful images.

The shapes have a simple structure that is amenable to deconstruction and reconstruction in ways that allow for discussion about generality.

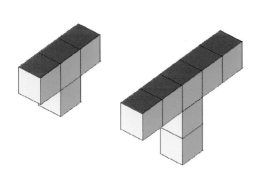

The picture alongside shows the first two members of a set of Tees.

Suppose you ask your pupils to think about the third member of the set. Would you want them to build it or use the structure implicit in the first two to identify its characteristics? If the latter then questions like this might be helpful.

- How many cubes will you need to make the arms?

- How many cubes will you need to make the stem?

- How many cubes will you need for the joint?

- How do the pictures below help your discussions?

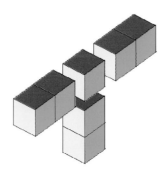 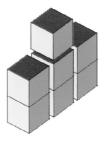

You could ask students to explore other letters like F, E, H or, C. Indeed, the letter C lends itself very well to the sorts of extensions which can be found on the L-shaped algebra pages.

1.3 Caterpillar Algebra

This is the last of the introductory activities. It came about one day when I was working with some year nine pupils on the factorisation of quadratics. A group of girls had made a family of caterpillars with each girl having a different member of the family on her table. One of these, for whatever reasons, came to be known as Cecil. Below can be seen the first three in a family of caterpillars.

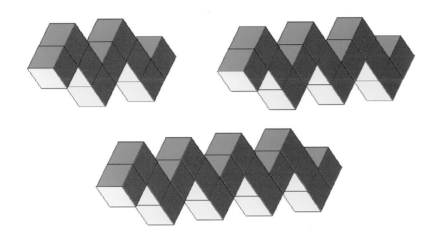

What could we say about the characteristic of the fourth caterpillar? Perhaps some deconstructions of the first might offer some insights.

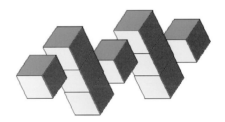

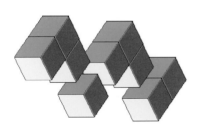

So if, for example, one looks at the first of these three images then one can see two inverted Ls of four cubes each plus a tail of one cube.

When generalised this structural image yields, for the nth caterpillar n+1 lots of the inverted Ls plus a tail of one cube. This gives $4(n+1) + 1 = 4n + 5$ cubes for the nth caterpillar. The other deconstructions give, apparently, different generalities and it is an entirely appropriate task to get pupils to try to reconcile those different forms as equivalent.

1.4 Ell-shaped algebra

This is another pre-algebra activity. It can be used to alert learners to notions of generality based on an awareness of those components that vary and those that do not. The role of the teacher is to facilitate discussion and to draw children's attention to the fact that each "L" has a structure comprising of, say, a vertical arm, a horizontal arm and a corner. The lengths of the arms correspond to the "n" value for that "L". Other structures are equally valid although I would like to encourage children to recognise and use symmetry when it's appropriate.

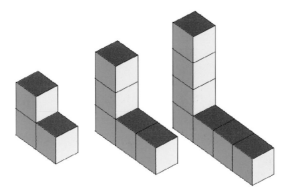

So, having offered pupils the image above of three Ls, one could invite them to make the fourth or attempt to describe its characteristics without recourse to manufacture. The latter process might include prompt questions like:

- How many cubes will you need for the corner?

- How many cubes will you need for the horizontal arm?

- How many cubes will you need for the vertical arm?

A similar conversation could consider the properties of the tenth L and, through oral descriptions, lead to an account of the general form.

Extension task

One of the exciting properties of the Ls is that one can create new sequences by putting consecutive Ls together as in the picture below.

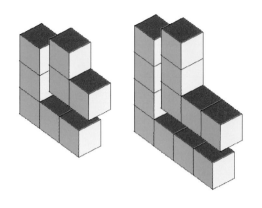

- What characterises these Ls?

- Are their properties the same or different?

- How any cubes will you need for their corners?

- How many cubes will you need for their vertical arms?

- How many cubes will you need for their horizontal arms?

- What form would the generalised L take?

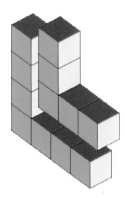

It is interesting that the sequence obtained from alternate Ls can be viewed in a variety of different but, ultimately, equivalent ways.

One perspective might be as follows. The second combined L can be seen alongside. It is a combination of the second and third Ls. Each combined L can be deconstructed and reconstructed in at least two ways.

The first, and perhaps, more obvious is shown in the picture below.

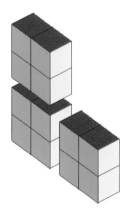 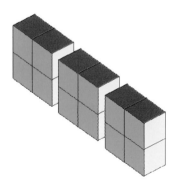

At the bottom left of the deconstructed picture one can see a constant square. Next to this are two arms of width two and, in this case, length two. More generally, the nth combination would have the same constant square (two by two) and two arms of width two and length n. Thus the nth combined L would comprise a square of 4 cubes and two arms of 2n cubes. That is, the nth combination will need 4n+4 cubes.

8

Alternatively, if one maintains the integrity of the original Ls then one can rearrange the two as shown below. That is the combined L can be seen as a square of side four minus a square of side two. More generally this is a square of side n+2 subtract a square of side n. That is, the nth combined L is equivalent to $(n+2)^2 - n^2$.

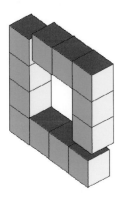

The nice thing now is to get learners to work on showing the equivalence of the two forms.

However, there remain many other avenues open to us. What if one were to create a sequence from three consecutive Ls? What about four, five....? What about the running totals?

In essence, there are many questions we could derive from a manipulation of the Ls. This would seem to suggest that pupils would need to have access to the cubes in order to construct and then explore their own ideas with respect to combining Ls.

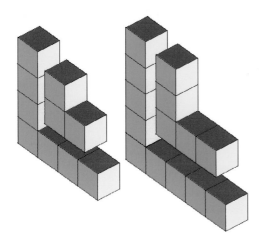

You could create a new sequence by combining alternate Ls and then, in addition to working on generalities prove that each of the new shapes is equivalent to a rectangle.

What if you varied the construction of the sequence in some other way? Try some for yourself and see where it might lead.

What if a new sequence was constructed thus:

$$L_4 + L_1, L_5 + L_2, L_6 + L_3, ...?$$

Investigate further. What would the general case be? The possibilities for getting pupils to engage with some algebraic manipulation seem almost endless.

2.1 The generalisation of triangular numbers

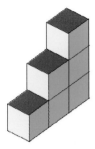 The following is an activity for helping pupils access the algebraic generality for the triangular numbers and through which the use of subscripts can emerge in a meaningful, and therefore successful, context. The task is premised on participants accepting the image alongside as representative of the third triangular number. That is, $T_3 = 6$.

It may be appropriate to spend some time, as a class, discussing why 6 is a triangular number and why it should be given the coding T_3 – it's the third triangular number, it has three rows and so on. The discussion is likely to involve many pupils and the making of different triangular numbers in order for what follows to make sense. The discussion is also likely to involve teachers making explicit not only the fact that the third triangular number is, of course, 1+2+3 but also that $T_4 = T_3 + 4$ and so on. This should highlight the general link between one triangular number and the next. More formally, although this is unlikely to bother the average twelve year old, this establishes the basis of mathematical induction.

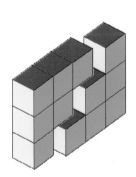 However, the main element of the lesson is to encourage pupils to place together two triangles of the same size. The picture on the left shows to T_3s which have been placed together to form a rectangle.

- What are the dimensions of the rectangle?
- How many cubes are in the rectangle? How do you know?
- How many cubes would there be in a T_3?

Once this has been done, one might invite pupils to try putting two T_4s or two T_5s together to see what emerges. Do two triangles of the same size always create a rectangle? Why?

From this discussion, which ought not to last too long, a sense of the generalised rectangle should emerge. That is, if two T_ns are placed together then a rectangle of dimensions n by n + 1 emerges.

Thus there are n(n + 1) cubes in the rectangle, which yields the desired formula, that the nth triangular number, T_n, comprises n(n + 1)/2 cubes.

2.2 Some facts about triangular numbers

The following activities are intended to encourage children to explore further the relationships between triangular numbers and, importantly, to explore and become familiar with subscripts and the generalities they frequently imply. In each case there should be an explicit expectation that the focus on the task is a generality derived from a structural analysis of the situation.

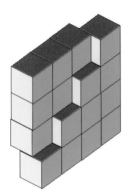

Activity 1: take any two consecutive triangles and put them together as shown alongside. In this particular case we can see that a T_3 has been placed on top of a T4.

What shape has this created?
Does this process always give the same result? Why?

What is the general result? That is, if a T_n is placed on top of a T_{n+1}, then what will be the result obtained?

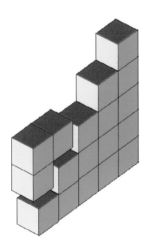

Activity 2: this is a more general version of activity 1. Take any two triangles and put them together as shown below. In this particular case we can see that a T_2 has been places on top of a T_5.

• Now what can be seen?
• What are the dimensions of the rectangle?
• Which triangular number is left on the top?

Try some other pairs of triangular numbers and see what you can find.

Generalise your results. That is, if a T_m is placed on top of a T_n, then what are the dimensions of the rectangle and which triangle is left on the top? Would your result still hold if you had placed the larger triangle on top of the smaller?

Show how the results of the last two activities are compatible.

Activity 3: the picture below shows how the fifth triangular number, T_5, can be split into a square and two equal triangles.

In the case below we can see that $T_5 = S_3 + 2T_2$

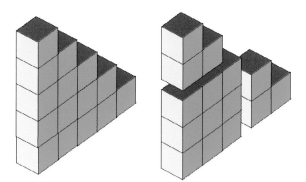

Investigate for other triangles. Is it always possible to get a square and two equal triangles?

Generalise the results - this is nice example where there is one rule for an even numbered triangle and one for an odd.

An interesting re-arrangement of the above dissection is shown below.

Is it always possible to generate a rectangle in this way?

If so, what would be its dimensions? That is, what would be the dimensions of a rectangle formed from the nth triangle, T_n?

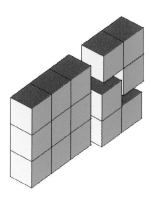

2.3 More facts about triangular numbers

The following explores some of the less well-known, yet equally interesting, results concerning triangular numbers. Take any triangular number, multiply it by 8 and add 1 to the answer.

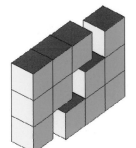

What do you notice about the result? What sort of number is it? Which one is it?

Try again with a different triangular number. Multiply it by eight and add one. What sort of number do you get? Which one is it?

How do the original triangular numbers, T_n, relate to the numbers you get as a consequence of multiplying by eight and adding one?

As with many other situations we could use standard algebraic manipulation on the general form of the nth triangular number to demonstrate the result.

That is, if $T_n = n(n+1)/2$ then $8T_n + 1 = 8n(n+1)/2 + 1 = 4n^2 + 4n + 1 = (2n+1)^2$.

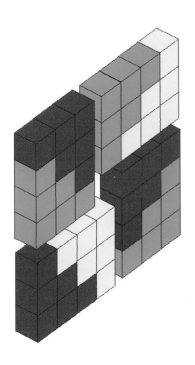

However, despite its obvious validity and, in a sense, algebraic simplicity I have no feel for its truth. I need to be convinced and it's here that linking cubes might help. For example, we know from previous pages that two T_3s can be placed together to form a rectangle of dimensions three by four.

Importantly, four of these rectangles can be placed to surround a one by one square, which shows that the dimensions of the square are two lots of three plus one by two lots of three plus one. Which, when one recalls that n in this instance is three, equates to a square $2n+1$ by $2n+1$ - the result we got from the algebra.

2.4 Triangles from triangles
(Difference of two triangles)

The activity below is intended to demonstrate how a reliance on number patterns as an approach to generalising sequences may not always be the most productive or insightful way of doing things.

Take two triangular numbers. We could, for example, take, say, 21 and 10.
Subtract the smaller from the larger. In this case we would get $21 - 10 = 11$.

$$\text{That is } T_6 - T_4 = 11.$$

A numerically-focused investigation would probably result in the construction of a table of values looking something like the one below. In this case we can see the triangular numbers, and their subscripts, along the outer edges of the table and the differences between them in the body of the table.

				m				
		1	2	3	4 T_m	5	6	7
		1	3	6	10	15	21	28
1		1 0						
2		3 2	0					
3		6 5	3	0				
n 4 T_n		10 9	7	4	0			
5		15 14	12	9	5	0		
6		21 20	18	15	11	6	0	
7		28 27	35	22	19	13	7	0

My guess would be that most pupils, when invited to find a rule for the difference between T_n and T_m, would struggle not only to find one that worked but also understand what they were being asked to do.

However, when approached from a structural perspective, the results become much less opaque. For example, suppose we wanted to subtract T_2 from T_6. We would be subtracting the smaller triangle below from the larger. This process, when done systematically and acknowledging the structures of the triangles, would give us images like this:

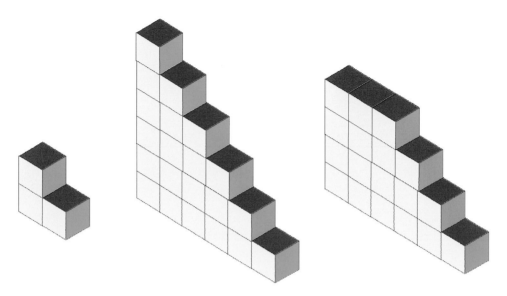

And when two of these are placed together, we get the picture below.

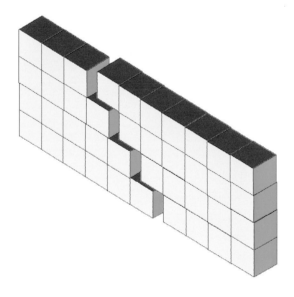

Now, the height of the rectangle is clearly n - m whilst the width is n + (m + 1)

Thus the number of cubes in the rectangle is given by $T_{n,m} = (n - m)(n + m + 1)/2$ where $T_{n,m}$ is the number of cubes left when T_m is removed from T_n.

2.5 Some identities concerning triangular numbers

Identity I

There are many identities concerning triangular numbers. Several are explored on some of the other pages. Those that follow concern the results obtained from operating upon them in systematic ways.

- Take any three consecutive triangular numbers, say 3, 6 and 10. Multiply the smallest and largest, square the middle one and <u>add</u> the two answers.
- So, in this particular case we get $3.10 + 6^2 = 30+36 = 66$.
- What sort of number is this? Which one?
- When considered in terms of subscripts the result above looks something like this: $T_2 T_4 + T_3^2 = T_{11}$.
- Repeat the process with other triples of consecutive triangular numbers.
- Generalise and prove your result.

Now, as with all such results, one could attempt to prove the generality algebraically. However, despite being a worthwhile consolidatory algebraic manipulation task for some learners, there is little insight to be gained from it. However, a geometric approach might be more informative.

Now, both the pictures above show the result of $T_2 T_4 + T_3^2 = T_{11}$. The one on the left is a consequence of arranging six (T_3) T_3s with three (T_2) T_4s. The one on the right comprises six (T_3) T_3s and ten (T_4) T_2s. Both arrangements are premised on the fact that the sum of T_2 and T_3 is a square (S_3). It is left to the reader to convince himself or herself that these arrangements will work for any three consecutive triangular numbers. Perhaps the images below will help:

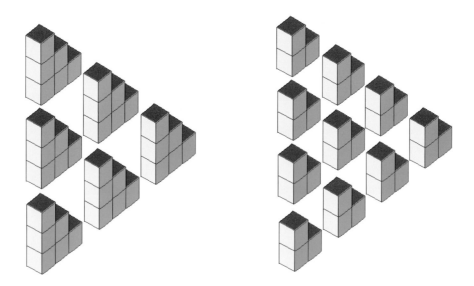

Both images are of the previous two but with those triangles that complete the squares removed. In both cases the triangles on the bottom rows are separated by a space left by a single cube. Thus the triangle on the left is $T_{3.3+2}$ whilst that on the right is $T_{4.2+3}$. More generally, if the three original consecutive triangular numbers were T_n, T_{n+1} and T_{n+2}, then we have two results.

$T_n T_{n+2} + T_{n+1}^2 = T_{(n+1)(n+1)+n}$ (from the left-hand image) or $T_n T_{n+2} + T_{n+1}^2 = T_{(n+2)n+(n+1)}$ (from the right hand image).

An additional task might be to check the equivalence of these two forms.

Identity II

A second identity can be obtained by means of a similar procedure.

- Take any three consecutive triangular numbers, say 3, 6 and 10. Multiply the smallest and largest, square the middle one and <u>subtract</u> the smaller answer from the larger.
- In this case we would get 3.10 = 30, 6.6=36, 36-30 = 6.
- When considered in terms of subscripts the result looks something like this: $T_3^2 - T_2.T_4 = T_3$.
- What would the general result be? Prove it.

As always there is likely to be a relatively straightforward algebraic solution which offers no insights. So, what might a geometric solution look like? In this particular case we wish to subtract $10T_2$s from $6T_3$s.

Now, $6T_3$s can be seen in the picture below, and when $6T_2$s are subtracted we get the second image which comprises six rods of length three.

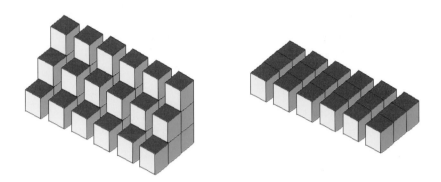

Now six is a triangular number so the six rods can be configured as in the picture below. This allows us to subtract a further three T_2s (making a total of nine T_2s subtracted so far) which leaves just a three by three square. Finally, the last T_2 can be subtracted by placing it over the square. This leaves just a T_3 as we had expected

Thus, if the three triangular numbers are T_{n-1}, T_n and T_{n+1}, we have shown geometrically that

$$T_n^2 - T_{n-1}T_{n+1} = T_n$$

Identity III

Take any four consecutive triangular numbers, say, 3, 6, 10 and 15.

21

Multiply the outside two. In this instance, 3.15 = 45. Multiply the inside two. In this case 6.10 = 60.

Add the two answers. Here we have 45 + 60 = 105.

In other words, we seem to have shown that $T_2T_5 + T_3T_4 = T_{14}$.

Now, as in all the cases we have considered before, I am confident that an invocation of algebra would lead to the general form, which could be proved by mathematical induction. Indeed, the left-hand side is equivalent to the following:

$$
\begin{aligned}
T_nT_{n+3} + T_{n+1}T_{n+2} &= n(n+1)/2.(n+3)(n+4)/2 + (n+1)(n+2)/2.(n+2)(n+3)/2 \\
&= (n^2 + n)(n^2 + 7n + 12)/4 + (n^2 + 3n + 2)(n^2 + 5n + 6)/4 \\
&= (n^4 + 8n^3 + 19n^2 + 12n)/4 + (n^4 + 8n^3 + 23n^2 + 28n + 12)/4 \\
&= (2n^4 + 16n^3 + 42n^2 + 40n + 12)/4 \\
&= (n^4 + 8n^3 + 21n^2 + 20n + 6)/2 \\
&= (n^2 + 4n + 2)(n^2 + 4n + 3)/2
\end{aligned}
$$

The last line shows the product of consecutive numbers, $n^2 + 4n + 2$ and $n^2 + 4n + 3$, divided by two which is the $(n^2 + 4n + 2)^{th}$ triangular number. This, when n = 2, gives T_{14} as we saw above.

However, this gives little satisfaction other than knowing one can perform appropriate algebraic manipulation. The interest lies in the insights that might be gleaned from the situation itself.

So, let's look at the geometry and see if the generality emerges.

Our original problem involved the four triangular numbers 3, 6, 10 and 15. We manipulated them and arrived at the fact that $T_2T_5 + T_3T_4 = T_{14}$.

Now, T_3 is a triangular number, which means it can be represented as a triangular array. Importantly, since T_4 is also a triangular number, the T_4 lots of T_3 can be presented as a triangular array of triangles. <u>This is shown below on the left.</u>

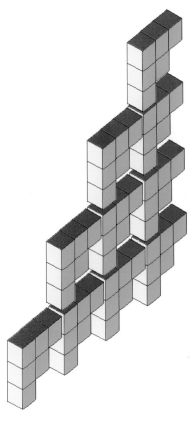

It can also be seen that there are gaps in the image that need filling if we are to show that we are to get the fourteenth triangular number. In fact, there are two types of gap - inside and outside the picture. Both are filled by the same shape - T_2. We need ten (T_4) to fill the inside gaps and a further five to fill the outside gaps. That is, we need fifteen (T_5) of the T_2 triangles to complete the picture.

This new shape can be seen below to the right. It is clear that it is T_{14}, the fourteenth triangular number. What is not clear, at least not yet, is why this should be the $(n^2 + 4n + 2)^{th}$ triangular number.

So, let's look at the picture more closely, bear in mind that in this particular case n = 2, and see what we can find out.

Put simply, the bottom row of the new triangle comprises the bases of five T_2s, each of which is of length n, plus the four cubes needed to fill the gaps between them. The figure five is significant in its being n+3 whilst the figure four is n+2. Thus the bottom row of the triangle comprises (n+3) lots of n plus n+2.

That is:

$$(n+3)n + (n+2) = n^2 + 3n + n + 2$$
$$= n^2 + 4n + 2$$

Which is the form we hoped to achieve.

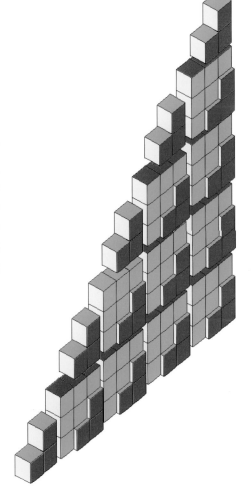

2.6 Cubes From Triangles

There are some very interesting identities concerning triangular numbers. Here is one.

Write down two consecutive triangular numbers. Square each of them. Subtract the smaller answer from the larger. What do you notice about your answer? Try again with two different consecutive triangular numbers. Generalise your result.

The answer is a perfect cube and this can be demonstrated algebraically by invoking some of the facts we know about triangular numbers. So, we have here, $T_n^2 - T_{n-1}^2$ and we know that

$$T_n^2 - T_{n-1}^2 = (n(n+1)/2)^2 - (n(n-1)/2)^2$$

Which can be manipulated quite easily to give n^3.

However, the invocation of algebra offers no satisfaction. There is no sense as to why triangular numbers manipulated in this way should give a cube. Why should the manipulation of two-dimensional objects in this fashion give a three dimensional object?

The following offers insights into the geometrical link between the numeric and the algebraic. But first, it is premised on our agreeing what squaring a triangular number might mean. You can see in the picture below three copies of the second triangular number, and in the picture next to it, six copies of the third triangular number.

My contention is that both pictures represent the squaring of the respective

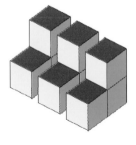
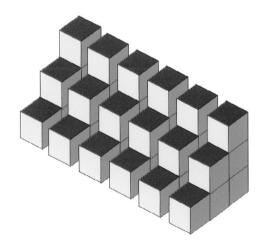

triangular numbers. Why? Can you convince yourself that squaring the third triangular number - which is six - requires six copies of the triangular representation?

Now, we are concerned with the difference between the two sets of figures. That is, in this particular instance, $T_3^2 - T_2^2$. The picture below emphasises what we might mean.

It can be clearly seen that subtraction can be represented by the systematic removal of the square of the second triangular number. This leaves:

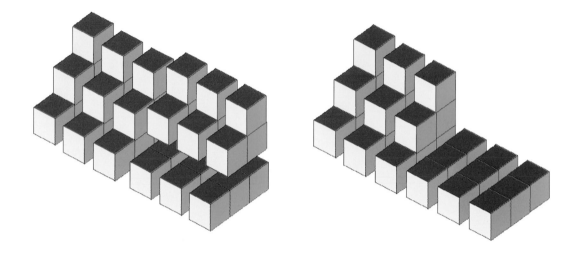

Which can be re-arranged to give the third cube.

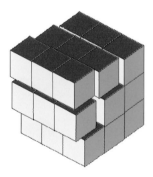

Convince yourself that this process would work for any pair of consecutive triangular numbers.

2.7 More cubes from triangles

The previous page on cubes from triangles has a delightful generality. We saw that the square of the third triangular number, that is T_3^2, can be represented thus:

And that this can be dissected, as shown above on the right, into three T_3 triangles, three T_2 triangles and three rods of length three.

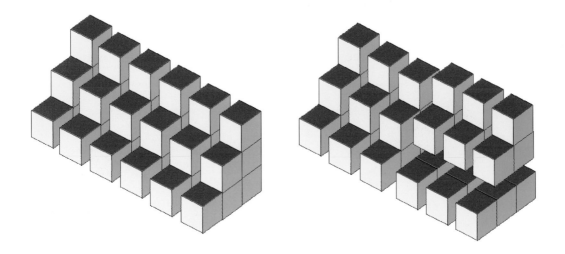

That is, instead of the original six pieces we now have nine, as shown below.

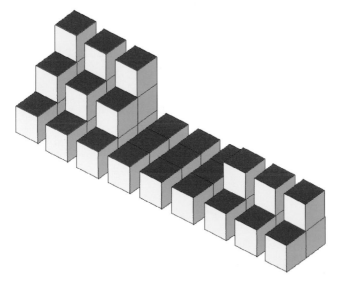

Of these, the six pieces on the left can be rearranged, as shown below, to form a cube. This leaves the three T_2s, which, of course, is the square of T_2.

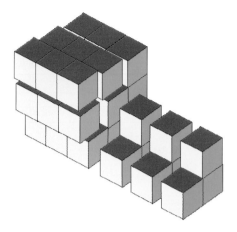

Now, we can operate on the three T_2s in a similar way to get the following:

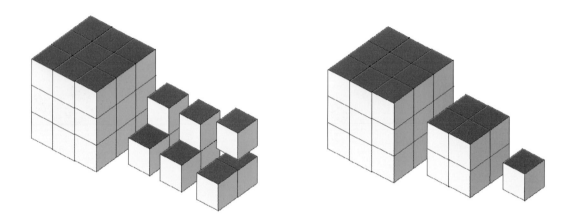

Thus we have shown that the square of the third triangular number (T_3) can be systematically shown to be equivalent to the sum of the first three cubes.

At this stage I would recommend that readers convince themselves that the square of the fourth triangular number is equivalent to the sum of the first four cubes.

That is:

$$T_4^2 = 64 + 27 + 8 + 1$$

Putting this all together we have demonstrated geometrically the identity

$$T_n^2 = \Sigma n^3$$

3.1 Squares and the sum of the odd numbers

The pictures below show the first set of a particular family of triangles. Without making it, decided what the next member of the family look like?

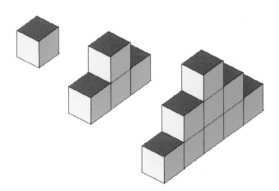

How many rows of cubes will it have?

How many cubes will you need for the bottom row?

What do you notice about the number of cubes in each row?

What do you notice about the total number of cubes necessary for the fourth shape?

Activities like this can be used to generate a variety of sequences. However, their usefulness derives from the insights which can be gleaned from them.

In this case the picture on the right might prove helpful.

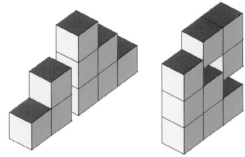

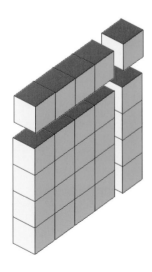

In essence, the point of this particular task is to alert learners to the different ways in which squares can be represented. In particular one would wish them to notice that a square is both the sum of two consecutive triangular numbers and the sum of the first odd numbers. Indeed, the structure of the latter can be seen below.

Importantly the diagram points towards the principle of mathematical induction and may be an appropriate activity for students' first steps towards it.

3.2 Squares on squares

The following task is not a lengthy one, nor should it be seen as anything other than a means by which learners might consolidate their understanding and awareness of the properties of square numbers. However, unlike other activities which have a very explicit structural underpinning, this is probably better seen as a means by which learners might develop the skills of systematic counting.

Invite pupils to make a square, say, of side length 6 - we can call this S_6. Ask them to make, also, a square smaller than S_6. S_2, for example, would suffice. Now invite them to find out how many different ways the smaller square could be laid flat on the larger square so that the cubes align. One such way can be seen below.

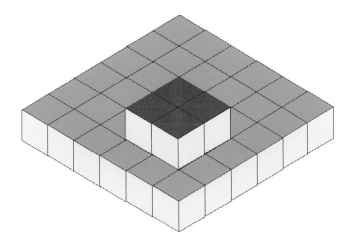

A variety of questions can be derived from this starting point.

- How many ways can an S_2 be placed on the same or larger square?

- How many ways can squares smaller than, or the same as, S_6 be placed on an S_6?

- What is the total number of ways that a smaller square can be placed on a larger?

31

How many ways can an S_2 be placed on the same or larger square?

The first question above is a particular example of the more general but allows for easier access. It's a question that encourages systematic counting. In some ways the structure of the task reduces counting to almost trivial levels, but for the novice there is some worth in its being pursued.

It ought to facilitate learners' development of an awareness that if the larger square has length n, then (n-1) S_2 squares can be placed along one edge of the larger square. Similarly, (n-1) S_2 squares can be place along a perpendicular edge, with the result that there must be $(n-1)^2$ places where an S_2 can be arranged on an S_n.

This particular investigation can then be continued for other squares - how many ways can an S_1, or an S_3 or an S_m be placed on a square of equal size or larger. The latter is interesting and leads to the general result that there are $(n-(m-1))^2$ ways of arranging S_m squares on top of an S_n.

How many ways can squares smaller than, or the same as, S_6 be placed on an S_6?

We have seen that there are 25 ways of arranging an S_2 on an S_6. But what of other small squares? How many S_1 squares can be fitted on an S_6? In essence, this second investigation might be used to derive the sums of the squares. This particular task can be used to introduce the more general idea.

What is the total number of ways that a smaller square can be placed on a larger?

This is just the generalisation of the previous two results. The sums of the squares idea can be seen on another page - see activity 6.2 on square pyramids.

Re-orientate the small square

An entirely new task emerges when we re-orientate the small square as shown in the

32

picture below.

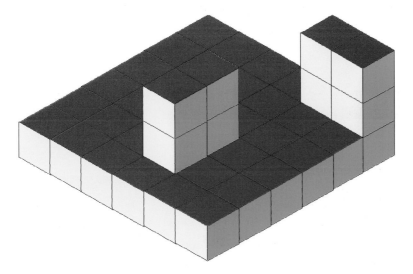

The rule concerning the alignment of cubes remains, but we get a different, and slightly less obvious, counting problem. Firstly we have to consider the small square in two orientations. Secondly we have to consider the fact the small square's footprint on the larger square is no longer square but rectangular.

However, the task is not difficult and ought to lead to some worthwhile algebraic manipulation based around similar reasoning to that described above.

Of course, the problem above is just another particular example of a more general problem. There is no reason, for example, why the small squares above should have a depth of just one cube. What if they were deeper?

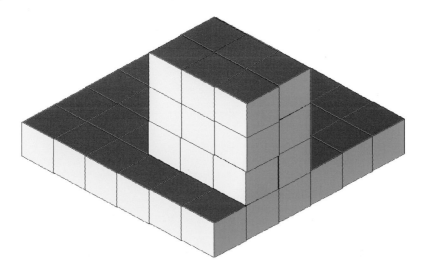

In the case shown here we have a large S_6 and an S_3 of depth 2. How many ways can this be arranged on the larger square. What would be the generalised result for an S_n large square and an S_m of depth d?

One would hope that by the time learners attack a problem of this nature, they would have acquired the skills of counting through systematic analysis rather than placing the one solid on top of the other.

By this I mean the following. In the orientation above the small square can be placed along the edge of the large square in 4 (6-(4-1)) ways. Also, the depth of the small square means that it can be arranged in 5 (6-(2-1)) ways along the perpendicular edge of the square. That means that this particular small square can be arranged, in this orientation, in 4 x 5 (20) ways on this larger square. Of course, symmetry would show that with the small square placed in the other orientation, there would be another 20 ways. Thus a total of 40 ways can be found.

This would generalise to $2(n-(m-1))(n-(d-1))$ ways.

3.3 Squares from squares

(Difference of two squares)

This activity is intended to help learners to make sense of what happens when a square is removed systematically from another. As will become clear, it also leads learners directly to the algebraic identity for the difference of two squares.

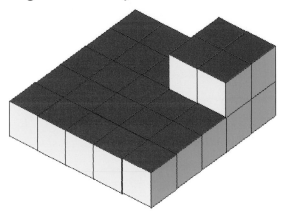

The picture above shows an S_2 placed on the corner of an S_5. The placing of one square on top of another in this fashion equates to an act of subtraction.

The number of cubes remaining uncovered is $25 - 4 = 21$.

As with all these tasks, teachers have to make decisions. Do they ask pupils to work through a set of such tasks in a systematic fashion or do they go direct to a more general solution.

In the former case, pupils will probably be invited to work through a set of tasks that culminate in a table of values that looks something like this:

Length of large square	5	5	5	5	6	6	6	6	6
Length of small square	1	2	3	4	1	2	3	4	5
Difference	24	21	16	9	35	32	27	20	11

However, the figures so derived are not particularly helpful in offering a transparent route to generality. Teacher intervention may be required. It would not be inappropriate, for example, for a teacher to invite learners to add further rows to the table. Something along the lines of

| Large length plus small length | 6 | 7 | 8 | 9 | 7 | 8 | 9 | 10 | 11 |
| Large length minus small length | 4 | 3 | 2 | 1 | 5 | 4 | 3 | 2 | 1 |

However, this amounts to little more than telling the learner what the rule is and, in some ways, negates the purpose of the exercise. Surely, as teachers, we are trying to set up tasks from which learners might infer a relationship in such a way that promotes relational understanding.

So, if we go back to the initial subtraction of an S_2 from an S_5, we can see the shape that remains below. Fortunately it is amenable to a systematic deconstruction and reconstruction, as the other images show.

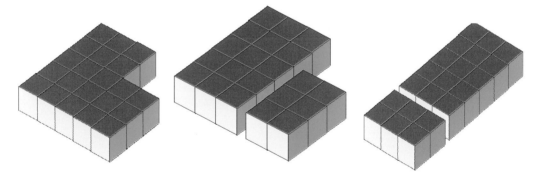

It can be seen from the deconstruction that if the length of the large square is L and the length of the small square is S, then the dimensions of the small rectangle in the centre image are S by (L - S).

Thus, the rectangle on the right has dimensions (L + W) by (L - W), which is the desired result.

3.4 More Squares from squares

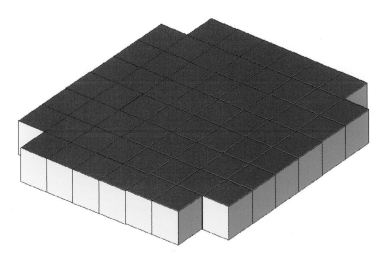

The picture above shows a square of side eight with the same small square removed from each corner. What is the largest square that can be removed from each corner and still leave some of the original square? How many cubes would remain?

More generally the question would become something like, given a square of side n, what is the largest square that can be removed from each of the corners and still leave something of the original. How many cubes remain?

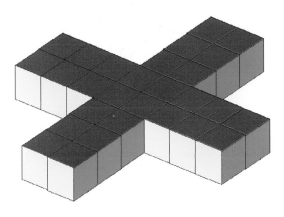

As can be seen from the picture on the left. If the starting square is of side 8 units then it is possible to remove four squares of side 3 and still have some left. In this case there would be 64 - 36 = 28 cubes.

As with all such investigations, learners could be invited to engage with a counting exercise. We would argue that a structural analysis is more productive and mathematically more appropriate.

It can be seen from the picture that a simple deconstruction of the remaining cross-shape gives a square and four rectangles. The edge of the square is two cubes - and will be for any even starting square (why?).

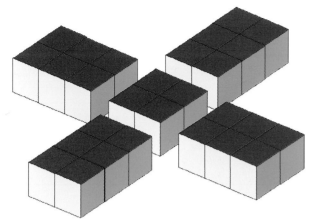

The dimensions of the rectangle are 2 (same reason as for the square) and (n-2)/2. Thus, we can see that for any even square the number of cubes that remain after the removal of four squares is 4 rectangles plus a square or

$$4.2.(n - 2)/2 + 4 = 4(n - 2) + 4$$

$$= 4n - 4$$

Of course, there will be a different rule for an odd square, but that is left for the reader to determine. Lastly, are the two rules - for odd or even squares - reconcilable or must they remain distinct?

Rectangles from squares

A variant of the same problem, but one in which rotational symmetry is invoked, explores the effect of removing the same rectangle from each corner of the original square with, of course, the proviso that some of the original square remains.

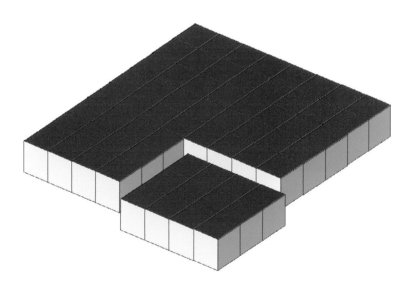

As can be seen from the picture, in the case of a square of side 8, one possibility might be to remove a rectangle of dimensions 3 by 4 from each corner.

38

- Is this the largest such rectangle?

- What is the rule that governs the size of rectangle removed?

- For a square of side n, what is the rule that determines the number of cubes that remain?

Developing the problem further: an obvious development would be to look at the largest rectangles that can be removed from the corners of rectangles or the largest cubes that can be removed from the vertices of a cube whilst leaving some of the original behind. For a cube of side n,

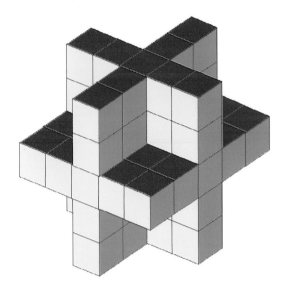

- What is the side of the largest cube that can be removed from each vertex whilst leaving something of the original behind?

- What is the rule that determines how many cubes are left behind

- What are the dimensions of the largest cuboid that can be removed from each vertex?

- What is the rule that determines how many cubes are left behind?

And, of course, these ideas can be developed further to consider the largest cuboids that can be removed from the vertices of a cuboid.

3.5 Rectangles on Rectangles

The picture below shows a rectangle of dimension 2 by 3 placed on a larger rectangle of 4 by 5. How many ways can the small rectangle be placed on the larger? Investigate further and generalise your results.

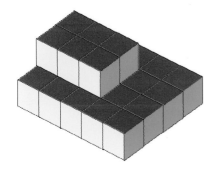

This investigation follows naturally from one earlier concerning the number of squares on a square and, it is argued, is a more general version. However, despite its generality, there is a surprising elegance to the solution to the question, how many rectangles can be placed on a rectangle of dimension m by n?

The solution can be achieved analytically or through a systematic count of the possibilities. In the example shown on the left, and with both rectangles oriented as in the picture, the smaller rectangle can be placed in 3 (4-(2-1)) by 3 (5-(3-1)), that is, 9 positions.

One can count, systematically, all the possible arrangements and then attempt to generalise. Indeed, such a task requires that the learner can systematise the process of counting in such a way that he or she is able to justify saying that the count is complete. In that sense, this is a better counting exercise than the squares on squares task because learners will need to make decisions for themselves as to how the count is structured. In the case above the total number of rectangles that can be fitted on the 5 by 4 rectangle is 150.

It is no coincidence that the answer 150, which includes squares (are squares rectangles?) is 15 by 10 where 15 is the fifth triangular number and 10 is the fourth triangular number. That is, for the case of a 5 by 4 rectangle, the total number rectangles that can be placed on top is T_5 by T_4, which of course, generalises to T_n by T_m for an n by m rectangle.

41

4.1 Staircases and Equivalent Forms

Below can be seen the first three of a sequence of staircases:

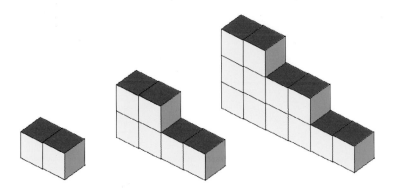

As with previous examples we can put two identical staircases together to form rectangles, which we can then generalise to give us the general form for the nth staircase.

However, as can be seen in the picture below, this can be done in two ways. We can construct either a long narrow rectangle or a short wide one.

Use each one to generalise the nth triangular staircase.

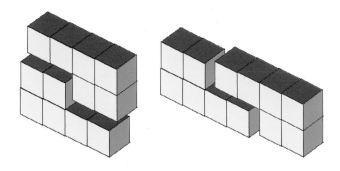

Try to explain why the two apparently different structures give the same generalisations. Why should they be equivalent?

4.2 Growing patterns

The pictures below show the first three of a set of growing shapes that can be made from linking cubes. Like most of the activities in this book, this activity can be

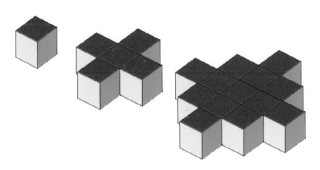

viewed in two ways. The one is a numerical investigation where learners count cubes, tabulate results and then generalise their findings, and the other requires the systematic de-construction and re-construction of each shape in order to tease out the general form.

The former could be addressed by means of questions like:

- how many cubes you would need for the fourth shape.
- how many cubes would you need for the tenth shape in this set.
- How many cubes would you need for the one hundredth shape?
- Write down how you would perform the calculation for any shape.
- How many cubes would you need for the nth shape?

Alternatively, each shape could be deconstructed and then reconstructed as shown below.

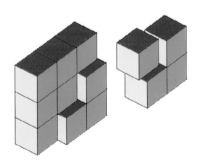 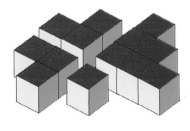

Can all such shapes be de-constructed and then re-constructed in this way? What is the general form?

4.3 Spirals

The intial activity below does not lead directly to a non-linear relationship. However, the latter do and in an interesting and accessible way. The pictures below show the first two members of a set of spirals. The task for the learner is to establish the number of cubes needed for the *nth* such shape.

 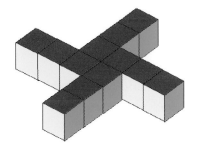

As in most of the tasks we have considered the learner is, in essence, presented with two approaches. The first could involve the tabulation of results and, hopefully, the identification of a generalised relationship whilst the other would focus on an invocation of structure. Indeed, a structural perspective might involve deconstructions something like those shown below.

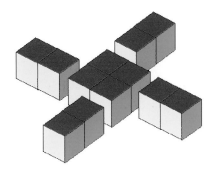 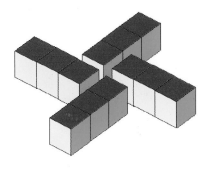

The image on the left comprises a square of four cubes, which is constant to all spirals, and four arms of length two. Thus, we can see that the nth spiral will comprise a square of four cubes and four arms of length n. That is, $4n + 4$ cubes.

However, the image on the right can be seen as four arms of length $n+1$, which yields a total of $4(n+1)$ cubes.

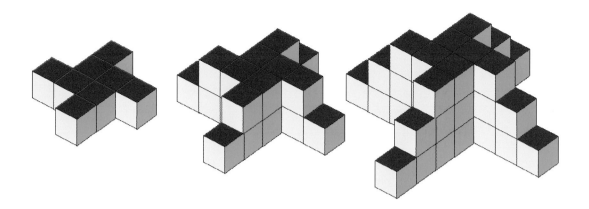

Another task altogether could be to consider the series formed from the sequence of spirals. For example, the pictures below show the first three such totals.

As with the earlier task one could count the number of cubes, tabulate the results and then attempt to generalise.

Tower Number	1	2	3	4	5
Total Cubes	8	20	36	56	80

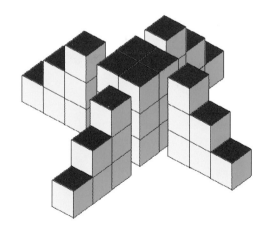

However, it may not be immediately apparent what the rule may be. It is my guess that a systematic deconstruction, as shown in the picture to the left, might help.

There are four triangles of height three (that is 4 times T_3) plus a column three cubes high with each row comprising four cubes.

Put algebraically, and acknowledging that $T_3 = n(n+1)/2$, we get the total number of cubes in S_n, the nth spiral, to be

$$S_n = 4n(n+1)/2 + 4n \text{ which factorises to give } S_n = 2n(n+3).$$

48

4.4 The Factorisation of quadratic expressions

Despite the fact that the factorisation of quadratic functions forms a significant element of the curriculum, few learners are ever made aware of the link between the algebraic and geometric forms of that factorisation. This activity alerts learners to those links in ways that make the algebraic identities transparent.

Let's start by way of an example. Suppose we want to factorise an expression like $x^2 + 3x + 2$. In essence the expression comprises three sets of components - the square, the three xs and the two units. We can represent each this set as in the picture below:

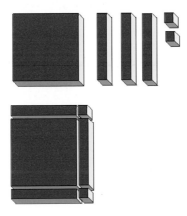

It can also be see that the pieces will fit together to form a rectangle - the dimensions of the rectangle can be determined from its structure.

$$\text{Thus } x^2 + 3x + 2 = (x+1)(x+2).$$

Pupils could be invited to try others of a similar vein - that is expressions involving only additions - and asked to infer a rule for the factorisation of such expressions. It might be appropriate at this stage to offer learners examples of quadratic expressions which do and do not factorise.

One way I have handled this activity with pupils is to get them to work in groups of, say, three or four. Each member of the group, after a brief discussion, is assigned a value for x - say 2, 3, 4 or 5. Each person then makes from the linking cubes their respective pieces. Each person attempts to arrange his or her pieces into a rectangle. However there is one rule which all group members must observe - each person's rectangle must have the same structure as every other person's in the group. That is, all members of the group must agree an identical structure for their rectangles and that this structure is independent of the value of x assigned to each student. This way the underlying structure can be drawn out.

Students could be invited also, to speculate as to what would happen if signs other than two positives were involved. For example, they could make conjectures, without attempting to make them, as to the factorisations of expressions like x^2+x-2, or x^2-3x+2 or x^2-x-2. Indeed, once they have made their conjectures they might like to show that there is a geometrically structural equivalence to their proposed solutions. These can be seen below:

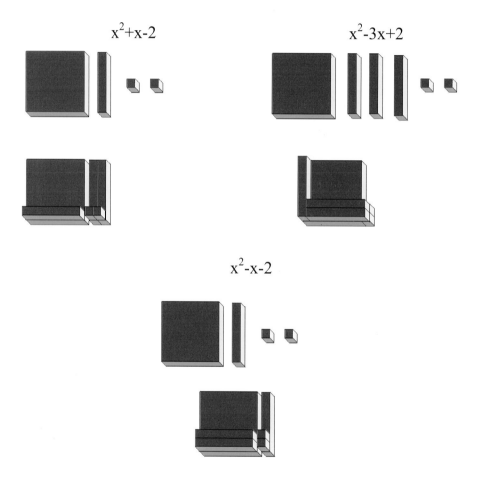

Several important points need airing. Firstly, teachers need to consider carefully how they use such ideas with children. My preferred option is something along the lines of the following "script".

I would encourage learners to explore trinomials involving positive terms only. From this they will generalise the process of factoring quite quickly - after, say, half a dozen examples.

Having generalised for positives only I would invite learners to make conjectures in respect of what might happen when negatives were introduced. That is I would hope they would use the rule already generated to make intelligent guesses as to what might happen - indeed, having made such guesses they can check their factorisations by multiplying out.

I would now use the linking cubes approach to confirm the conjectured relationships. I acknowledge that the task is not a simple one and many people may have some, transient, difficulties. However, if learners persist with the cubes then they are more likely to notice the structural integrity of algebra than those who do not.

In summary the approach is to use the cubes to investigate quadratics with positives and to generalise. The rule is then used to make conjectures for quadratics involving negatives which can then be tested with the cubes.

There are other issues. Firstly, the picture below shows a factorisation for a more generalised quadratic relationship. That is $2a^2 + 3ab + b^2$.

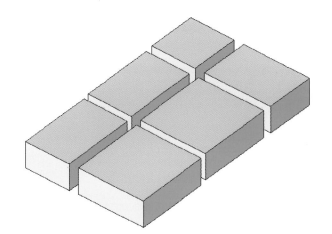

This begs a fairly important question. Should I, the teacher, begin my work on factoring with this generalised form and then alert learners to the particularities of expressions in just one variable, or do I continue, as I have in the past, to start with the simple case?

I am not convinced that there is a simple answer to this question.

4.5 Linear sequences and their series

The following activities are offered in the form of a sequence of ideas. Throughout a structural emphasis is employed in the hope that learners will begin to generalise both the individual sequence and series and, importantly, recognise the wider generality that is implicit within any particular linear sequence.

The activities are not intended to be used as they are presented here. Teachers will need to work on how they would wish to use them with their students; the questions they might wish to ask and the manner in which the tasks are presented.

Linear Sequences

Consider a linear sequence like 1, 4, 7, 10, ... What are the properties which we may wish to exploit in order to encourage children's greater understanding of the sequence and its construction? How might we use these properties to facilitate their being able to generalise? Does the picture below help?

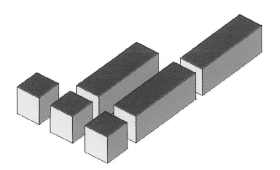

What would be the structure of the tenth term in the sequence? What about the fiftieth or nth?

Try some others. What about 2, 6, 10, 14,...., or 3, 7, 11, 15, or 5, 8, 11, ...

More generally, if the first term in the sequence is a, and each successive term is the result of adding d to the previous term, then the nth term of the sequence is the sum of a and (n-1) lots of d.

That is, if u_n is the nth term, $u_n = a + (n-1)d$

Series I

Now, by making running totals from the sequence above, a series can be formed. The first three terms of the series can be seen below.

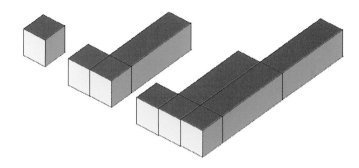

In this particular case we get the series 1, 5, 12, ... Of course, this is still a sequence but its construction is that of a series which may demand that we look at it in other ways.

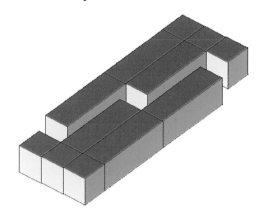

What if two identical pieces are placed together as above? Is a rectangle always created? What are its dimensions? Do the dimensions generalise?

What does this tell us about the number of cubes in the nth term of the series?

In its most general form one could describe the width of the rectangle as n, the number of terms summed, and the length as 2a plus (n-1)d.

Thus, if S_n denotes the nth sum, or term in the sequence, then twice the sum is equal to the rectangle.

That is, $2S_n = n(2a + (n-1)d)$, giving, $S_n = n(2a + (n-1)d)/2$.

Series II

Now let's repeat the process. What if were to make a new series from the last one? What would we get? In fact the solid below shows the sum of the first four terms of the original series.

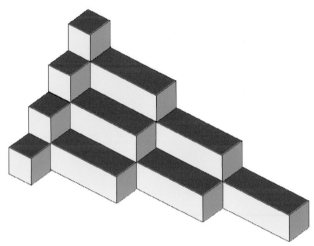

Does this yield a reconstruction which might help us generalise the nth term? Do we have any insights from earlier work?

One can see that the solid appears to comprise the fourth triangular number, T_4, and a "stretched" triangular pyramid of the type found on the page "pyramids from triangular numbers".

However, the triangular number we see is also stretched as a consequence of the first term of the original sequence being a rather than just 1.

Thus the solid comprises T_4 multiplied by a (to account for the stretch) plus the third triangular pyramid multiplied by d.

Now, the nth triangular pyramid was found to be $n(n+1)(n+2)/6$ and the nth triangular number was $n(n+1)/2$. But, we want the $(n-1)^{th}$ pyramid - because the solid is the fourth and the pyramid shown here is the third.

Putting all this together gives the following for the nth term, S_n, of the series.

$$S_n = an(n+1)/2 + d(n-1)(n)(n+1)/6$$

$$= n(n+1)/2.(a + d(n-1)/3)$$

5.1 A cubic problem

The picture below shows a cube made from 13 rods of two cubes, as shown, plus a single cube. Each rod comprises the same two colours. Here they are red and yellow.

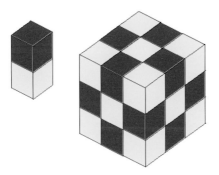

Each face of the large cube, as shown in the picture, is identical and has the appearance of a chess board.

The initial task is to find a way of putting together all the pieces to make the larger cube. This is an accessible spatial activity and one that lends itself to different structural approaches which learners, both children and adults, can be invited to share.

A problem like this also offers some interesting opportunities for accessible work on proof and justification and, in addition, provides an activity for introducing learners to the cubes themselves.

Some questions that come to mind, all of which require explanation, are:

- What colour is the single cube?

- What position does it occupy?

- Is the solution unique?

- Can you make a cube of length two from such rods?

- What other questions might be constructed around rods and cubes?

5.2 Frames from cubes

The activity below is less concerned with algebra than it is with proof. It is my experience that too many students go through their mathematics lessons without ever really getting to grips with the nature of, or need for, proof.

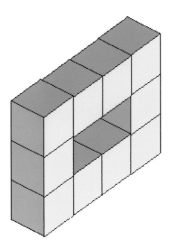

The picture above shows a *rectangular* frame. The task for learners is to prove that every such frame must contain an even number of cubes. In general pupils often offer different proofs and it can be interesting to compare them.

This particular task can be used as an introduction to mathematical induction in the sense that the result can be proved by means of an inductive form of argument.

Extension

There is an extension which some learners, both adult and children, may find challenging. It involves their being asked to construct closed frames with five, six, seven, eight or more sides.

When they try to do this learners will notice that some are possible and others not. At this point they should be invited to prove why some can and others can not be made.

5.3 Closed cornered circuits

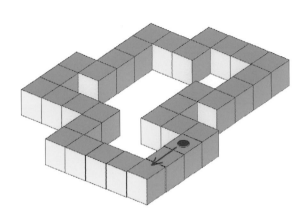

The picture alongside shows a circuit made from linking cubes. The circuit has fourteen sides (edges) and fourteen corners (vertices). Count them to check that this correct.

Starting at the marked cubes, and travelling in the arrowed direction (clockwise), take a journey around the circuit.

How many right turns do you make? How many left turns do you make?

Repeat the process for different circuits - travel clockwise and count the number of right turns and left turns. Some questions that spring to mind are

- What can you say about the number of sides and why?

- What can you say about the number of left turns?

- What can you say about the number of right turns

- What is the rule that determines the number of left and right turns for a circuit of n sides

- What would happen to these rules if your journey went anti-clockwise?

This particular task, whilst not difficult to solve, is of interest because it is one of a set of similar such tasks that allow for an inductive proof before learners need to engage with the formalities of mathematical induction. That is, it is a task that allows learners access to the principles before burdening them with the syntax.

Consequently, one would hope to see learners being encouraged to attempt a proof to their rule based on an examination of the different transformations of the simplest circuit. For example, the simple circuit below can be made more complicated by transforming an edge. The results of this can be seen in the picture below on the right.

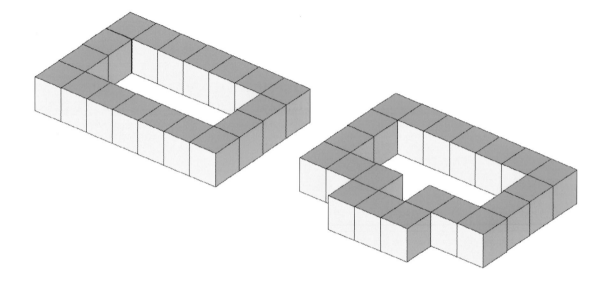

- What effect does this transformation have on your rule?

- Is it the only transformation of an edge? What others could there be?

- Is it possible to transform a corner? How and what effect would this have on your rule?

It is hoped that the totality of the arguments above show that there is a demonstrably provable rule for the number of left and right turns for a closed circuit and that this helps learners become familiar with inductively constructed proofs.

5.4 The four cube and other problems

The point of this activity is to familiarise pupils with linking cubes and to encourage the development of the skills of three-dimensional drawing based on isometric paper. However, there are some significant mathematical issues implicit in the tasks which grants them a validity that mere colouring could not.

Invite pupils to find as many different solids as they can that can be made from four cubes. There is an issue here for teachers. If your pupils are novices at working on relatively open questions they may find this a difficult task and need a different form of introduction - you may prefer to suggest to them that there are eight such solids and that their task is to find them. In other words - the success of such a task will be determined, in part, by both the experiences of the learners and the manner in which the problem is posed to them.

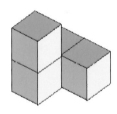 One such solid is as shown alongside. As indicated above, there are eight solids which can be made from four cubes. Most children will find seven relatively quickly. Their difficulty, if they have one, will arise from their failure to recognise that the solid on the left is different from that which is obtained when the image is reflected in a vertical axis.

When pupils have found all eight solids they can be invited to try one of several tasks according to what you, their teacher, have decided is the objective for the lesson.

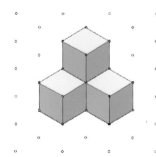 Task 1: pupils could be invited to draw each of their solids on isometric paper as an introduction to 3-D drawing as shown alongside.

Task 2: pupils could be invited to arrange all eight solids into a cuboid (how many ways can this be done?) and then to show their arrangements on an exploded diagram on isometric paper.

Task 3: pupils could be invited to explore how each of the five "flat" solids can tessellate the plane and, consequently, be used to fill space.

Task 4: using as many or as few of the solids pupils could be asked to construct as many cuboids as possible - what are the possible dimensions? How many are possible and how many ways can each be done?

5.5 Surface area

This problem interests me because it allows for different levels of access. At one level we can address the question, what is the maximum surface area we can achieve by linking n linking cubes? This might lead to an exploration of the number of such solids for any given number of cubes. It should certainly lead to questions which encourage children to engage with justification and proof.

Take four linking cubes and link them together. One possible example is shown below.

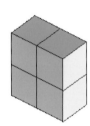

What is the surface area of your solid, in the case shown here the surface area is 16 units squared?

What is the maximum surface area you can achieve with four linking cubes? How do you know this is the maximum?

Investigate further with different numbers of cubes.

What is the rule that determines the maximum surface area for any number of cubes?

Extension task: for any given number of cubes, how many different solids can be made with the maximum surface area? For example, some of these solids for four cubes can be seen below:

 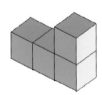 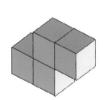 

What others might there be?

Thus far we have focused our attention on the more obvious result concerning the maximum surface area for a solid of n cubes. This last task looks at the minimum. The generalisation is not necessarily straightforward but it is there and forces the learner to abandon the belief that algebraic rules always follow a simple linear or quadratic form.

What is the rule that determines the minimum surface area for any number of cubes? Why?

5.6 Surface area and skeleton cubes

The activity offered below is probably more difficult than some of the others found in these intermediate pages and there are times when I am tempted to think of it as a more advanced activity. However, this uncertainty raises, for me at least, the perennial question of relativism. What does one mean by an advanced activity? Is it determined by the mathematical content it is intended to address or by the level of thought necessary for its completion? I am not necessarily convinced by either proposition and tend to find myself concluding that distinctions as to the level of a piece of work are arbitrary and more likely to act as a barrier to, rather than a facilitator of, learning.

The solid below is a skeleton cube made from linking cubes.

You are offered a series of tasks to consider, each of which allows for a relatively straightforward generality based on a structural examination of the solid.

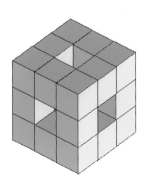

Task 1: how many linking cubes are needed for its construction? What would be the number of linking cubes for a skeleton cube of edge length n?

Task 2: what is the surface area of this skeleton cube? What would be the surface area of a skeleton cube of edge length n?

Task 3: how many linking cubes would be needed to fill the faces of the skeleton cube above? What would be the number necessary to fill the faces of a skeleton cube of edge length n?

Task 4: how many linking cubes in the skeleton cube above have two faces hidden by other linking cubes? How many linking cubes in a skeleton cube of edge length n have two faces hidden by other linking cubes?

We can also look at skeleton cuboids.

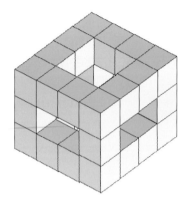

Task 5: how many linking cubes are needed for the construction of the skeleton cuboid on the left? What is the rule for the number of linking cubes needed to build a skeleton cuboid of dimensions length (*l*) by width (*w*) by depth (*d*)?

Task 6: what is the surface area of the solid shown? What would be the surface area of a cuboid of dimensions *l* (length) by *w* (width) by *d* (depth)?

Task 7: how many cubes would be needed to fill the faces of the skeleton cuboid above? What would be the number necessary for a skeleton cuboid of dimensions *l* by *w* by *d*?

Task 8: how many linking cubes in the skeleton cuboid above have two faces hidden by other linking cubes?

How many linking cubes in a skeleton cuboid of dimensions *l* by *w* by *d* have two faces hidden by other linking cubes?

What other questions could one ask? What about the solids formed by the interiors of these skeleton cubes and cuboids? The picture below shows the interior solid formed from the skeleton cuboid above.

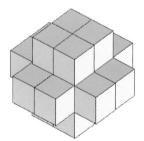

Task 9: what is its surface area of this solid?

What would be the surface area of a solid formed from the interior of a skeleton cuboid of dimensions *l* by *w* by *d*?

5.7 Trapezium numbers

The picture below shows a trapezium constructed from linking cubes. In some ways it could be seen as an extension of the squares from triangles activity. It has three rows and the top row comprises five cubes. The rules for construction are that there must be at least two rows and that each row has two cubes more than the row above it.

There are several questions we could ask of something like this. These might include:

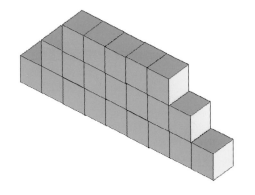

- how many cubes would there be in a three row trapezium with *n* cubes on the top?

- how many cubes would there be in an *m* row trapezium with *n* cubes on the top?

- what numbers can not be expressed as trapezia?

- which numbers can be expressed as trapezia and in how many ways?

These all seem to me to be worthwhile questions although, as is indicated below, the first may be less relevant than the rest.

How many cubes would there be in a three row trapezium with *n* cubes on the top?

This question could be addressed in a variety of ways and I am ambivalent as to which might be the more appropriate. Traditionally learners will be invited to build a collection of such solids in order to collect data for tabulation. The more I think about such activity, the less convinced I am that individual pupils should be making them all – it probably makes sense for teachers to task allocate such work within a group. One child makes a trapezium with two on the top, another makes one with three on the top and so on. Our intention is to exploit the structures, not to spend too long on making them. Once tabulated pupils will normally be invited to work with the number patterns in order to derive some form of generalised statement about the family of trapezia with three rows.

Thus, we might see a table like this one:

Cubes on top row	1	2	3	4	5	6	7
Total cubes	9	12	15	18	21	24	27

Pupils with experience in this form of working will be able to see that the rule for the nth trapezium will be determined by the constant difference of three, leading to the result that $T(\text{otal}) = 3n + 6$.

Such an approach could be repeated for trapezia of four rows, five rows, two rows and so on. However, as has been said before, there is little satisfaction to be gleaned from such an approach in terms of personal conviction. Why is the result $T = 3n + 6$. This is where the invocation to a structural analysis comes in.

The picture above can be rearranged as shown below on the left which is then transformed to the image on the right, which confirms what we obtained from the pattern spotting exercise. That is, there are five (n) rows of three (number of rows) plus a rectangle of dimension 3 (number or rows) by 2 (number of rows less one).

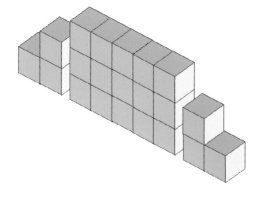 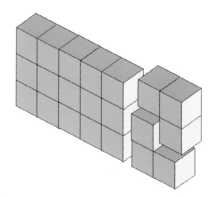

How many cubes would there be in an *m* row trapezium with *n* cubes on the top?

Clearly, an problem like this one is more concerned with a higher level of generality than just trapezia with three rows. What if it had *m* rows? The process of deconstruct and reconstruct can lead to an interesting set of insights.

The first is a shown in the image above. If the trapezium has m rows and n cubes on the top row then the total number of cubes is given by $T = mn + m(m-1)$.

Alternatively, we could argue that we have derived a single rectangle of height m and length n + (m-1). This would give $T = m(n + m - 1)$.

However, there are other interesting deconstructions, as can be seen below:

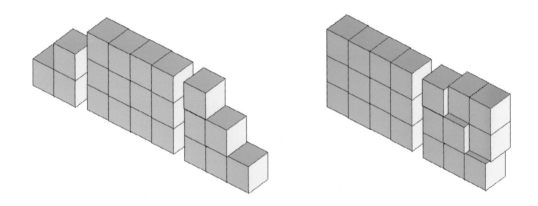

And it can be seen here that the total number of cubes is a rectangle comprising *m* rows of *n*-1 cubes plus a square of side *m*. That is $T = m(n-1) + m^2$.

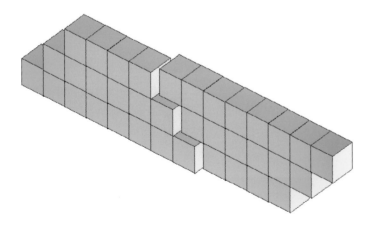

Of course, another way of generalising trapezia would be to place two together as shown on the left.

The base of the parallelogram is the sum of the base of the trapezium and the number of cubes, *n*, in the top row of the trapezium. Because each successive row contains two additional cubes and because there are *m* rows, the base of the trapezium is always n plus n plus (m-1) lots of 2.

71

Thus the number of cubes in the parallelogram is m(2n+ 2(m-1))

Which gives m(n + (m - 1)) for the trapezium

These are pleasing results because they now needs to be reconciled with the earlier.

What numbers can not be expressed as trapezia?

If you try to do it, you will find that some numbers seem impossible to express as trapezia. For example, you will probably have found that 4 is the smallest one you can make. You may also have found that you can not make 5, 7 or 11. What are these numbers? We can prove the result relatively straightforwardly, providing you understand factorisation.

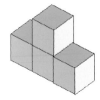
The two results obtained so far share the same factorisation of T = $m(n - 1 + m)$. Now, since a trapezium has to have at least two rows (that is, m is never less than two) and that n can take any integer value, the smallest value that the bracket in our expression can take is 2. This occurs when $m = 2$ and $n = 1$ and corresponds to the smallest possible trapezium.

This tells us that the rectangle we have derived can never have a length or width of one unit. Alternatively, it tells us that the rectangle we get is always the product of two numbers which are greater than or equal to two. This proves that a prime can never be represented as a trapezium.

As indicated above, there are other questions that could be asked. However, as far as this page is concerned, they remain to be answered.

5.8 Consecutive Sums

One of the most interesting investigations concerns those numbers which might be represented as the sum of consecutive integers. The picture below shows, for example, how 15 can be expressed as the sum of three consecutive integers $4 + 5 + 6$. The only rule, and this is implicit in the use of the word sum, is that there must be at least two numbers in the sum. The activities are accessible to learners of all ages and abilities. There is no expectation that they should be undertaken in a linear fashion although it could be argued that coherence would be achieved if they were done over several years. A task such as this can take several forms depending on the teacher's objectives. Among these could be, for example,

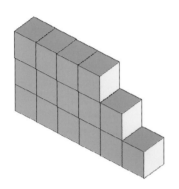

- Which numbers can be formed from the sum of two consecutive numbers?

- Which numbers can be formed from the sum of three consecutive numbers?

- What is the rule for the nth number formed from the sum of three consecutive numbers?

- What is the rule for the nth number formed from the sum of m consecutive numbers?

- Which numbers can not be represented as the sum of consecutive sums?

Which numbers can be formed from the sum of two consecutive numbers?

The picture alongside shows two images of seven (the fourth odd number) placed together to form a rectangle. In this case the rectangle's dimensions of seven by two are a consequence of the length being four plus three ($n + (n-1)$).

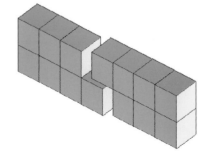

This shows that the number of cubes in the rectangle is $2(n + (n-1)) = 2(2n-1)$,

which shows that the nth odd number is $2n-1$.

This is a question worth asking as it reinforces the fact that all odd numbers can be so represented and raises the question as to whether zero is odd or even.

Mathematical induction and numbers formed from sums of three consecutives

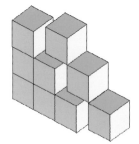

One issue worth exploring relates to the process of mathematical induction. Learners will soon see that six is the smallest integer representable in this fashion and that each new three-sum number will be the previous plus three. Consequently, one statement we can prove is that if the first number representable as the sum of three consecutives is a multiple of three then all such numbers must be.

Admittedly this argument lacks the formality of the accepted form of an inductive proof, but the purpose here is to alert the learner to the principle rather than the syntax. There are other problems that illustrate the principle just as well. However, learners find induction problematic and it is my conjecture that this could be ameliorated by exposure at an early stage to such activities.

What is the rule for the nth sum formed from three consecutives?

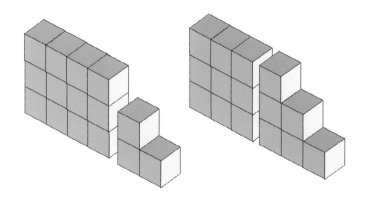

As can be seen from the images alongside and below, there are several ways that fifteen as a sum of three consecutives can be viewed from the perspective of deconstruct and reconstruct.

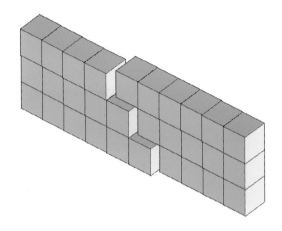

We can see from the first image that if n represents the number of cubes on the top row then the nth sum, S_{3n}, of three consecutive numbers would be given by $S_{3n} = 3n + T_2$, where T_2 is the second triangular number, 3. That is, $S_{3n} = 3n + 3$.

The second shows $S_{3n} = 3(n - 1) + T_3$ or $S_{3n} = 3(n - 1) + 6$.

The third image shows that $2S_{3n} = 3(2n + 2)$, giving $S_{3n} = 3(n + 1)$.

The fact that each result looks different allows for a meaningful discussion on their equivalence through its placing such work in context.

What is the rule for the nth number formed from the sum of m consecutive numbers?

All three of the above images can be seen as particular representations of the more general. In the first case, the nth sum of m consecutive numbers would be given by

$$S_{mn} = mn + T_{(m-1)} = mn + m(m - 1)/2$$

In the second case we would have:

$$S_{mn} = m(n - 1) + T_{(m)} = mn - m + m(m + 1)/2$$

In the third we would get

$$2S_{mn} = m(2n + m - 1) \text{ which shows that } S_{mn} = m(2n + m - 1)/2$$

which, of course, is the sum of the first m terms of an **arithmetic progression** with first term n and difference 1.

Which numbers can not be represented as the sum of consecutive sums?

This is one of the most intriguing results to which school-based learners might be exposed and for which aspects of the proof are accessible. The only numbers which cannot be represented as the sums of consecutives can be found through a process of trial and improvement.

The first, and most obvious, such numbers are one and two. Further investigation shows that neither four nor eight will fall. This leads to the natural conjecture that powers of two cannot be so represented.

The proof of this conjecture is, in essence, a proof by contradiction and is premised on the assumption that powers of two can be represented as consecutive sums. That is, we assume that powers of two can be of the form $m(2n + m - 1)/2$, which is the general rule we found above for the nth member of the sums of m consecutives.

The first thing we note is that the powers of two can have no odd factor other than one.

Case 1. Let m and n be even. In this case it can be seen quite clearly that the bracket in this case would yield an odd number. Also, because m is even, $m/2$ is an integer. Thus, when m and n are even, the consecutive sum has an odd factor.

Case 2. Let m be odd and n be even. In this case, the bracket returns an even number because m-1 becomes even. Thus the bracket divided by two will return an integer leaving the m outside the bracket as an odd factor for the expression. Thus, when m is odd and n is even, the consecutive sum has an odd factor.

Case 3. Let m be even and n be odd. In this case the bracket returns an odd because $2n$ is even and $m-1$ will be odd. Also, because m is even, $m/2$ will return an integer. Thus, when m is even and n is even, the consecutive sum has an odd factor.

Case 4. Let both m and n be odd. In this case the bracket will return an even number because both $2n$ and $m-1$ will be even. Thus the bracket divided by two will return an integer leaving the m outside the bracket as an odd factor. Thus, when both m and n are odd, the consecutive sum has an odd factor.

Thus we have shown, that in every case, the expression for a consecutive sum will have an odd factor which allows us to conclude that powers of two cannot be represented as consecutive sums.

Two additional questions that relate to the above are

- Can all other numbers be represented as consecutive sum?

- How many ways can such numbers be represented as consecutive sums and how is that total determined?

6.1 The skeleton tower

The activity below, as with most of the activities presented on these pages, requires that teachers will need to work on their understanding of the algebra embedded within it. I hope, for example, that teachers will encourage children to exploit the structural properties of a tower in order to justify any general statements they make about them. I do not deny that counting cubes and tabulating results is a valid mathematical activity itself but there is such a delightful (which is not a unique perspective) structure to the towers that not to exploit it would seem a pity.

In essence two tasks are offered. The first concerns the number of cubes on the bottom layer of a tower; the second addresses the total number of cubes in any tower.

Below are the first three members of set of towers. Make them from linking cubes.

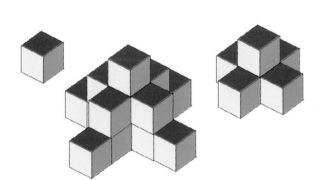

Now, try to answer the following questions without making any more towers.

How many cubes would you need for the bottom layer of the fifth tower?

How many cubes would you need for the bottom layer of the tenth tower?

Write a sentence explaining how you would calculate the number of cubes needed for the bottom layer of any tower. Generalise.

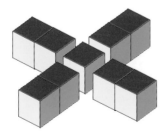

Does the picture above offer any insights? The first picture shows the bottom layer of the third tower. It has four arms, each of length two and a single centre cube. This generalises to $4(n-1)+1$.

Suppose you wanted to find the total numbers of cubes in any tower. The pictures below might help. Will this process always yield a rectangle? is the generalised result?

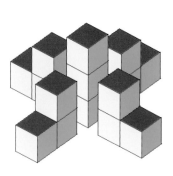 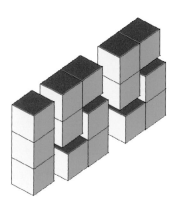

A different skeleton tower

The picture below offers a variation on a theme.

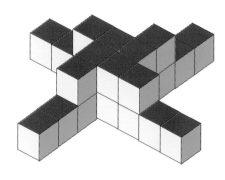

- Can this tower be reconstructed into a rectangle in the same way?

- If so, what are its dimensions?

- What would be the generalised rectangle?

- How many cubes would be needed for the nth tower?

6.2 Square numbers and their pyramids

(sums of squares)

This activity makes accessible to all learners, irrespective of age, one of the identities usually only shown to older students of mathematics. That is, the identity for the sums of the squares.

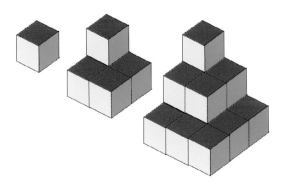

Above are three pyramids and each one is, effectively, the sum of consecutive square numbers. Students could be asked to make them from linking cubes.

In small groups they could be invited to do the following. One group could be asked to make six of the second pyramid. Another could be asked to make six of the third pyramid and so on.

The task is to arrange six identical pyramids to form a cuboid. Students can then be asked to consider the dimensions of the cuboid. From this they might generalise the dimensions in relation to n, the size of the pyramid.

Once the cuboid has been generalised the number of cubes in the nth pyramid can be obtained by dividing the general form for the cuboid by six.

79

The task is not difficult, although some learners will find arranging the six pyramids more difficult than others. The only prerequisite is that students are familiar with the idea of generality and have the skills and understandings necessary to generalise the cuboid in terms of n. It can be seen that in the particular case above, the generalised cuboid has dimensions, width n+1, height n, and length 2n+1.

Therefore the number of cubes in the cuboid is $n(n+1)(2n+1)$ giving us the fact that if P_n represents the nth pyramid then

$$P_n = n(n+1)(2n+1)/6.$$

The role of the teacher in asking appropriate questions is, however, fundamentally important to the success of the task. Significantly, the role of the teacher in alerting children to the generality of the particular case is also fundamental to the whole process.

An activity like this provides is a contextualised opportunity for pupils to show on isometric paper how their six solids fit together.

It is also an opportunity for them to engage with explaining how they know that the six solids will fit together without leaving any space unfilled. Such solids form 3-D tessellations which is probably unexpected by most learners and might form the basis of a conversation about space filling.

6.3 Triangular numbers and their pyramids

(Sums of triangles)

The picture below shows the third member of a set of pyramids made from triangular numbers. It can be made in several ways as the diagrams next to it indicate.

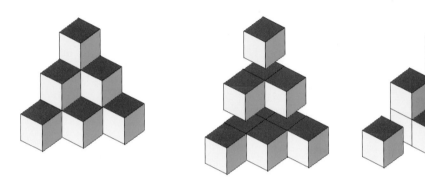

However, if our objective is to find a geometric means by which to generalise the nth such pyramid we have to transform each pyramid in a systematic way that preserves the integrity of its structure. The pictures on the right show two simple transformations of the centre of the above three images.

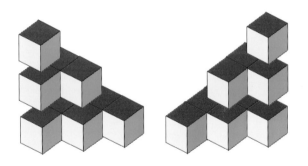

And these, when put together, look like the solids below.

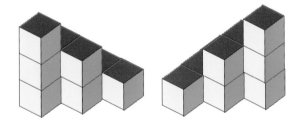

Now, you need to make three of each of these transformed pyramids - to give you six in total. Once you have done this you should be able to put the six transformed pyramids together to make a cuboid.

Hint: try putting two of one and one of the other together first. Then do something similar with the remaining three. Lastly, the two parts should fit together neatly. Something like in the picture below:

The picture has been shaded in such a way as to make more obvious the structure. Importantly, it is the structure that will give us the general form for the nth cuboid.

In this particular instance we have the third cuboid - because it is the result of putting together six transformed copies of the third pyramid.

We can see by inspection that the cuboid is three cubes high, by three plus one (4) cubes wide and three plus two (5) cubes long. Generalising, we can see that the dimensions of the nth cuboid would be n by n+1 by n+2.

Thus six copies of the nth pyramid yield a cuboid of n(n+1)(n+2) cubes.

Thus, if P_n denotes the nth pyramid, we have $P_n = n(n+1)(n+2)/6$.

6.4 Generalising pyramids

The following relies on the learner having worked through several of the earlier tasks. These include *Squares and the sums of odd numbers (3.1)*, and *Square numbers and their pyramids (6.2)*.

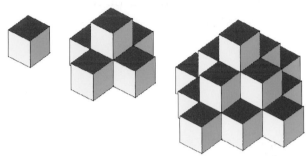

The pictures on the right shows the first three of a growing set of pyramids.

Without making it, calculate the number of cubes you would need for the fourth pyramid. How would you generalise the result?

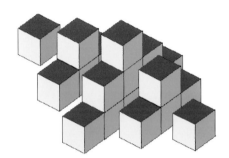

One can see that each pyramid can be split (deconstructed) as shown on the left. That is, a structural analysis shows that it is the sum of a set of triangles.

However, as can be seen below, each triangle is equivalent to a square.

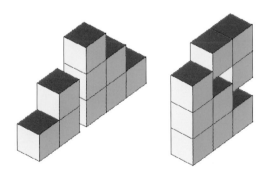

Which tells us that the pyramid on the previous page is equivalent to a sum of five squares. This, as shown on the right, can be transformed into two square-based pyramids.

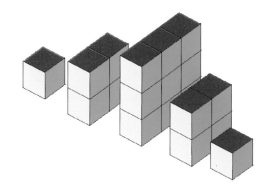 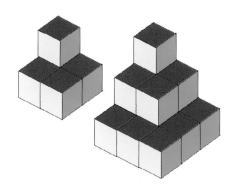

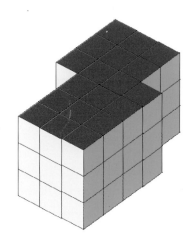

Now, we know, from the work we did on *square Pyramids*, that six copies of each square-based pyramid fit together to form a cuboid. So, thinking along similar lines, we could see whether three of the large and three of the small square-based pyramids fit together.

Interestingly they fit together as in the picture on the left, which, as can be seen below, is equivalent to two cubes plus a column.

Therefore three of our original pyramids are equivalent to twice n^3 plus n. That is, if the nth pyramid is described as P_n then

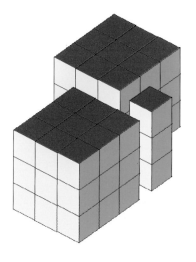

$$3P_n = 2n^3 + n.$$

$$\text{or, } P_n = (2n^3 + n)/3.$$

7.1 Talking mathematically

This is a simple activity that cam be used to help in the development of children's abilities to talk mathematically. In general the activity is most successful when they work in pairs although, should there be an odd number of pupils in the class, a single three should be unproblematic.

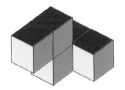 The following share a common theme in that one pupil makes a solid from five cubes – an example can be seen alongside - which is unseen by the other, who then attempts to make the same solid according to different rules.

Activity 1: pupils sit back to back with their cubes in front of them. The first pupil makes a model and explains to the other how it is made. The second tries to make it but is not allowed to challenge or query what is said by the first.

A variation of the first activity would allow the second person to challenge what the first has said.

Activity 2: pupils sit back to back and one makes a solid. The second is allowed to ask questions of the first to which he or she may answer only yes or no. In this way the second pupil should be able to construct the same model as that made by the first.

Activity 3: in this variation pupils sit face to face, one makes a solid behind his or her back and then explains to the second pupil who makes it behind his or her back.

Activity 4: as above, pupils sit face to face. One makes a solid and then helps his or her partner to make the same solid by responding either yes or no to questions posed by the other.

Of course, there is no reason as to why only five cubes should be used or different variations not tried.

7.2 Probability

This activity can facilitate pupils' understanding of the link between classical and frequentist conceptions of probability. That is the convergence of a repeated trial to the definition resulting from an equally likely outcomes analysis of a situation.

In my experience it helps for pupils to work in pairs. Each pair is given a small bag – the bag needs to be opaque - of cubes of two different colours. As a rule the total number of cubes in a bag would be between, say, eight and twelve with, preferably, the numbers of the two colours being co-prime. Thus, for example, one bag might contain five of one colour and four of another, a second bag might contain three of one and seven of another and so on. In this way a set of different bags can be made available.

The initial task is for pupils to draw a cube, record its colour and replace it in the bag. This experiment is then repeated nine times. At the end of this process, pupils should be invited to predict the likelihood of either of the two colours being drawn. This repetition of ten selections is repeated, say, a further four times to give fifty trials in total. After each set of ten, pupils should be invited to revise their predictions.

At the end of this sequence pupils can be invited to make a conjecture as to the probability of a particular colour being drawn should a further trial take place. Once this has been done pupils might open the bag and count the two sets of cubes in order to test their conjecture against the reality.

Each pair of pupils can then repeat the process with a different bag.

The intended outcome for a lesson like this is for pupils to see how the outcomes from a repeated trial approximate more closely, as the number of trials increases, the predictions of classical probability. It is suggested here that linking cubes provide an appropriate context for such work.

7.3 Sampling

The activity outlined below can be used to develop children's understanding of sampling as a statistical technique and be used as a context for either the teaching, or the consolidation, of a variety of other statistical processes.

The task is best undertaken in small groups of, say three of four pupils. Each group is given a plastic carrier bag containing a large, but unspecified, number of cubes of a single colour. By large I mean something of the order of two or three hundred cubes. Each group would have a bag of a different colour.

The bag is intended to simulate a lake and the cubes represent a species of fish in the lake - although this is but one of many possible contexts for simulation. A discussion is held with the class, to establish the need to conduct a count of the fish in the lake – the reasons for this could be many, one of which might be to see whether numbers are dropping as a consequence of, say, a pollution incident. The discussion should be managed in such a way that pupils will realise that the count cannot be managed by emptying the bag and counting the cubes – this would be equivalent to emptying the lake and killing all the fish. Eventually someone will mention that taking some samples might help, but, of course, taking samples from a bag containing cubes of only one colour is unlikely to yield information of any value. At this point it would be helpful if someone were to suggest introducing a known number of cubes of a different colour – this would be equivalent to introducing a marked population of fish into the lake.

Pupils can now introduce into their bags a known number of a different coloured cube and be invited to do some sampling. This will require further conversation as yet more issues will need to be resolved. This might include questions like

How many cubes are removed for each sample?
How many samples should be made?
How will the results to be analysed and interpreted?

Tasks such as the one described here can be attempted at a range of levels – they can be accessible to young learners as the basis for teaching elementary statistical techniques and they can be used with older pupils as the basis for distributions.

A variation would be to offer a bag containing large numbers of two different colours – the authorities need to maintain a check on the gender balance in the lake.

7.4 Permutations and combinations

The activities on this page could be done with almost any objects. The advantages to be gained with linking cubes derive from the following

- they come in a variety of colours which facilitates understanding
- their linking together helps in the recording of permutations and combinations
- they are small and portable
- individuals or small groups can have sufficient to make complete records of their work
- the activities shown here can be used with learners of any age which means that they can have an informal exposure to such ideas before they reach them formally

Activity 1: learners are invited to take four cubes, each of a different colour and to find the number of different rods of length four can be made such that each is coloured in a different order from the other.

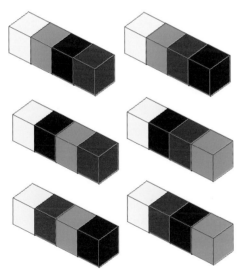

The hope is that colleagues will engage in conversations with their classes in order to draw out notions of system. For example, in the picture on the left there are six rods with a yellow on the left-hand end. If the rods are arranged according to a system learners will be able to see that the total number of ways in which four cubes can be arranged will be equal to four - because there are four colours which, in turn, can be placed at the left hand end of the rod - multiplied by the number of ways in which three cubes can be arranged.

Now, the number of ways in which three cubes can be arranged can also be seen in the picture above - ignore the yellow cube and it is clear that this amounts to six ways.

The responsibility of the teacher in a situation like this is to decide which tasks need to be set to which learners. Should they first be invited to see that three cubes can be arranged in six ways?

Should they be asked to consider the number of rods that can be made from five cubes, each of a different colour? The strength of the latter task is that the number of arrangements with five cubes begins to get large and beyond where I, as a teacher, am usually prepared to allow my students to go. The activity takes too long and is an ideal opportunity to invite them to consider what would happen if one colour were fixed at one end of the rod.

Whatever decisions colleagues make, this activity can be used to derive the idea that the number of arrangements that can be made from n cubes, each of a different colour, is $n!$

Activity 2: learners are invited to work on the number of rods of, say, length three from collections of four, five, six different colours. This task shifts their attention from the use of a complete set of cubes, as in activity 1, to the use of a subset of cubes. This process, if discussed sensibly, can lead to an awareness that the number of rods of length m, when drawn from a set of n different colours, is $n!/(n-m)!$

Activity 3: this repeats some of the above but with colours being duplicated. The precise nature of the tasks is clearly the decision of the individual teacher, but questions like how many rods of length four can be made from

- a set of four different colours?
- a set of four with one colour repeated once?
- a set of four with one colour repeated twice?
- a set of four with two colours repeated?
- a set of four all of one colour?

might be helpful starting points.

Activity 4: this leads to combinations rather than permutations. In the previous tasks the order in which the cubes were arranged mattered and led to permutations. With combinations, the order does not matter with the consequence that any two rods made from the same cubes would be defined as equivalent. A useful way of distinguishing derives from the idea of a committee - a committee of six people remains the same committee irrespective of the order in their names are written.

Thus a suitable starting point might be a question like, how many committees of three can be selected from a group of five people?

Some closing thoughts

I hope you have found this book useful from both professional and personal perspectives. I would be delighted to think that you have enjoyed it and learnt something new about mathematics and some of its stunning and enigmatic structures. All teachers operate within a curricular framework of specified learning outcomes and objectives. I hope that the activities in this book will help colleagues address those objectives in ways that allow learners not only to understand mathematics more deeply but encourage a delight in the aesthetics of the subject.

However, this is only the beginning. It would be fantastic to share other ideas with interested colleagues. It would be marvellous to see more learners engage, both mentally and physically, with images that alert them to the structural properties of mathematics and from which generality and proof might emerge. To this end, I invite you to share any ideas and tasks that you use with your students that involve the use of linking cubes. As you will have seen from the book, linking cubes can make substantial contributions to the learning of many topics at all levels of the curriculum, so, whatever the focus of your tasks, I am sure they will be of enormous help to others.

It would be tremendous to think that we might, together, develop a second compendium of activities. Clearly any publication will depend on colleagues' willingness to engage in the sharing process, knowing that the outcome will depend on there being sufficient tasks and activities to justify the ATM's collating and printing them. I hope there will be and, clearly, would acknowledge any contribution used. Should you wish to contact me about this, or any other matter concerning the book and its content, my email address is paulandrews@atm.org.uk I would be delighted to hear from you.

Lastly, should any school or local authority wish the ATM to provide a course on the use of linking cubes in the teaching of mathematics, it would be delighted to do so. In this regard, please contact its Professional Officer, Barbara Ball, via email: barbaraball@atm.org.uk, or the Association's Derby office on 01332 346559.